After the Storm

Poems on the Persian Gulf War

Edited by

Jay Meek & F. D. Reeve

MAISONNEUVE PRESS
Washington, D.C. 1992

Jay Meek and F. D. Reeve, editors. *After the
    Storm: Poems on the Persian Gulf War.*

Copyright © Maisonneuve Press
    P. O. Box 2980, Washington, D.C. 20013

Acknowledgments: please refer to the last
page of this book which constitutes a
continuation of this copyright page.

Maisonneuve Press is a division of the Institute
for Advanced Cultural Studies, a non-profit
organization committed to promoting research
in contemporary culture.

Printed in the U.S. by BookCrafters,
Fredricksburg, VA

Cataloging in Publication Data

After the storm : poems on the Persian Gulf
    War / edited by F. D. Reeve & Jay Meek.

      p. 122 cm.
    ISBN 0-944624-16-2 (paper) : $10.95
    1. Persian Gulf War, 1991 — Poetry.
    2. American Poetry — 20th century.
    3. War poetry, American.   I. Reeve, F. D.
    (Franklin D.), 1928 — . II. Meek, Jay.
PS595.P46A38 1992   92-11673
811'.54080358   92-11673   CIP

R. A. Clark

◄
◄   **"After the Storm"**

Contents

Illustrations

After the Storm—

By Way of Introduction

*Sing, goddess, the anger of Peleus' son Achilleus
and the devastation . . .*

—famous words, the opening of the *Iliad*, what Simone Weil called
"The Poem of Force," the Western world's first great war poem now
some 3000 years old. At its center is glorious Achilles, handsome,
strong, artistic—the embodiment of mankind's talents and virtues.
Three times in the poem he symbolically dies; so, we foreknow that
some time after the two months' warfare described in the poem, not
only will the Achaians sack Troy but also Achilles will finally die.
We understand that in time even war ends, but so does triumphant
man's strength, beauty, and grace.

The chain of slaughter that comprises the poem's combats praises
and honors the victors for courage, pride, stamina, acumen—in short,
manliness. By the time the poem was written down some four
centuries after its composition, thoughtful men understood that in
the bloody, human quest to imitate the immortal, bloodless gods
victory was illusory—*La grande illusion*, as the French film 2500
years later was titled.

The twelve-part Mesopotamian *Epic of Gilgamesh*, dating from
the third millennium before our era and written down some 1500
years before the *Iliad* begins—

O Gilgamesh, Lord of Kullab, great is thy praise.

—but wall builder, animal hunter, devil slayer and
vigorous womanizer Gilgamesh runs up against his own
mortality, confessing—

Because of my brother['s death] I am afraid of death

—and begins a search for everlasting life. The quest leads him to
Utnapishtim, a human made immortal by the gods, who tells
Gilgamesh:

> From the days of old there is no permanence. . . . Life
> and death they [the judges and the mother of destinies]
> allot, but the day of death they do not disclose.

Betrayed by a snake, Gilgamesh dies exhausted, and the poem
impassively, with self-conscious irony, closes as it began:

> O Gilgamesh, Lord of Kullab, great is thy praise.

When we set the history of war in the frame of civilization, we
see that one characteristic predominates. Victory after victory,
regardless of medals and ribbons and all individual incentives and
rewards, the course of a war and the 3000-year pattern of human
warfare express ever greater destruction. The fact is that war
dehumanizes.

The Peloponnesian War destroyed Athens. Henry V's boyish spirit
on the eve of Agincourt was echoed by Britons in August 1914, but
instead of winning a game, they defeated the Germans and lost an
empire—their own. The more powerful the weapons used, the greater
the damage done and the less significant the soldiers who use them.
3000 years ago, the shield of Achilles was crafted by one super-smith
and carried by one super-man; in our time, thousands of men and
women are involved in producing and dropping one bomb. Indeed,
the *agon*, or one-to-one combat among citizen heroes of the Trojan
War, became mass movements of mercenaries in the Roman and
Ottoman empires, then from the Renaissance through the 19th
century, three- and four-day pitched battles among conscripts and,
in the early 20th, a four-year trench war leading to the contemporary
concept of total destruction. Modern warfare is an effort to kill
everyone and everything, exemplified by the American bombing of
Dresden in 1943, of Hiroshima and Nagasaki in 1945, of the villages
of Vietnam during the decade 1964-1974, and of Iraqi cities in 1991.
Because by his skill Achilles alone killed Hektor, he takes full glory—
and responsibility—for it. Airmen who drop bombs are integers in
a system, do not think their enemy human, claim no responsibility.
Far from glorifying them, their roles emphasize their replaceability
and their individual insignificance.

War is no longer one man against another, or—regardless of
politicians' lies—good versus evil, but life against death. The more
we war, the more we kill those on the other side and those on our
side. Many Iraqi men, women, and children died in the Gulf War,

which, like the invasion of Panama and the war in Vietnam, failed. American soldiers died, many from "friendly fire." The ostensible objectives of establishing peace in the Middle East and removing Saddam Hussein from power were not achieved. Instead, just as the Vietnam War demoralized America and the invasion of Panama left cocaine flowing freely into the U.S., so Saddam Hussein thumbs his nose at America from a region whose political and ecological equilibrium has been severely shaken. Billions of dollars have been wasted that still are needed for health care in America, for debt reduction, a new energy policy, and for the elimination of poverty. Worse than the expensive parades and superficial patriotism of American militarism are the re-explosions of racism, the imposition of conformity by violence, the corruption of language, and the perversion of cultural ideals and values. Pointing at the naked emperor, that is what the poets of *After the Storm* are saying.

They are not self-righteous. Some recall Marianne Moore's "In Distrust of Merits"—

> There never was a war that was
> not inward:

—see some fault in human nature that "causes war." Others see the Gulf War in sequence to our presence in Nicaragua and El Salvador, and to our attacks upon Grenada and Panama, another misadventure calculated to pump up support for our military and to oppress third-world countries. Even before Vietnam, Robert Lowell had foreseen in "Waking Early Sunday Morning" how our children would die

> in small war on the heels of small
> war—

Saddam Hussein and the Kuwaiti royals remain entrenched in their positions of power. We won what? No longer believing in anything, lusting for the feel of winning, we simply stopped distinguishing spectacle and hype from actual events, which, even so, were often obscured from view.

Several poets here have written poems on the spectacle of televised war, broadcast live from the front as if it were a sport. As disastrous as the war was to people in the Middle East, back home the spectacular presentations of nightly devastation dulled us to suffering and helped millions prepare for the smugness with

4

which we celebrated the war's end, even as thousands of Kurdish refugees lay slaughtered by Iraqi forces. Who can calculate the great hurt we are done, failing to comprehend the pain of others, failing to understand that our staged triumphs and parades come on the backs of hundreds of thousands caught in such sordid fictions as this war became?

All conflicts war on language, with language. During these weeks in late winter, each briefing gave us a new avoidance, a phrase to ease our tolerance for killing—"surgical strikes," "incontinent ordnance," "ballistically induced apertures"—to wash the dead in the Baghdad bunker, or along the road to Basra. What remained were the burning oil wells in Kuwait, sludge that threatened the Gulf ecosystem, land mines lying buried in the desert heat, unstable, waiting to go off.

There is little as comfortingly heroic as the exercise of civility in the midst of war and its atrocities. One thinks of Wanda Landowska in Paris recording Scarlatti sonatas while in the background anti-aircraft fire sounded, cut into the groove; Fritta in Terezin drawing the horrors of the Nazi work camp with implements and paper taken from his captors; Issac Stern in Jerusalem returning to the stage after the air-raid alarm went off to play a Bach saraband before an audience in concert dress and gas masks. What can match such grace?

For the poets writing here there is no better way to affirm the integrity of our language than by giving us poems that will not tell lies. By their work, they demonstrate that the fictions handed out to us are inadequate to our lives, and that even as our government pulls away from us, we can affirm the democratic process by speaking out against the mass joviality and compliance that pose an inward danger to the heart.

Jay Meek
F. D. Reeve

John Aleshire

Ithakas

> Wise as you will have become, so full of experience,
> you'll have understood by then what these Ithakas mean.
> —Cavafy

(for Jesse D., February, 1991)

You said that a poem
you'd carry with you always,
the one addressed to you—
"Hope your road is a long one"—
in praise of the marvelous journey,
the one Odysseus took after his
world war. Is it on you now?
Sand filling the folds of the paper
I'd typed it on, your sweat seeping through
when you ride closed in hot metal, wind
erasing the tank's tracks as they're made.

Your father told me how you ran to him
where he worked in the field,
shouting you'd joined, you'd joined,
as if you'd been part of nothing
before. You put your name
to the contract with no hesitation
when the recruiter handed you his pen.
Seventeen, taking the straight road,
leaving our messiness and uncertainty behind.
Have you had your first earthquakes yet—
the fear, the wound, the trigger's thrill?

Hope your journey is long
the Greek poem says, and I do,
but I want it differently: an Ithaka
gained without going to war, or going
anywhere. A destination found daily
before you, tending the ground
around olive trees, for example,
not rushing through. An Ithaka
watching the fruit reach ripeness.
Harming as little as you can.
Ithaka the right time to crush
the olives, finding in their oil
an ingestible light.

Dick Allen

Breaking the Truth

Walk around it at first. Inspect it for cracks
And discolorations. Shoo the crows from it,

The nude sunbathers, the scholars, the poets
Who love it by instinct. At night

Flood it with prison spotlights, send across
Its wild terrain your surplus helicopters

And middle age heroes. When you've constructed
An adequate map, call on the engineers

With their explosives. Learn to lay charges
And stand far back. Once you've begun

To fissure and gully and shatter it,
Take care not to stop. Use sledgehammers,

Pickaxes and shovels. Have your best soldiers
Guard against looting. Beware any peasant

Who reads books too deeply, any worker
Singing to her fellows of a lark or sparrow.

Keep your priests exiled. When it is rubble
Go at it the harder, reduce it to dust,

Scatter the dust in the ocean. Only then
Will you feel safe from it, will you sleep well

Until (for it is Truth) it arises again
Beneath your palace window, huge and whole,

Covered with flowers. Use machine guns this time,
Poison its rivers. Pock the land with your lies.

John Allman

The Destruction of the Tower in Khafji

Molly's atop the TV,
    black tail dangling in counterpoint
to the tower where Iraqi
spotters call in fire upon the marines
who are knocking holes through a cinder-block
wall,
        a long swaying comma
      where the colonel talks,
      helmet strap tight under his jaw,

a phone ringing until our answering machine
blares, offering free estimates on vinyl
                siding.

Molly curls into herself
as high-rise apartments lose
their stucco look, lathing shredded
and hung like lace underwear,

marines taking howitzer hits,
Qatari tanks with erect cannons
moving on Khafji the announcer describes
as beautiful by the sea.

Molly looks over her shoulder,
annoyed the blanket next to us
is crumpled. She turns to the window,
    pupils wide with darkness,
spotting a purple finch that flutters
    in the ivy clinging to the house,

her pink lips trembling,
ech ech ech ech ech,
mimicking birds,

                awaiting
summer's crisp cicada,

the monarch slowly flapping,
the soft head of the white-footed mouse,

the evergreens on Young Road draped with yellow
bows,

my student's essay denouncing Olaf glad and big.

A graphic shows the convoy near Wafra
hit by B-52's, animated gray clouds
    appearing and disappearing
like exploding trucks in a Road Runner cartoon.

Molly,
      disgusted with the finch
      that has fumbled in the ivy and flown away,
drops heavily onto the carpet she marked last year,
leaking urine—

a burned personnel carrier, its front wheel
twisted like a broken leg in its boot,
side-wheels crusted and huge as an earth-mover's,
bits of slab embedded between thick treads,
a door wrenched from its hinges the idea of
door,

      Molly now on her back,
staring at us upside-down,
her white belly like trapped fluff
blown from the dryer,

the colonel clenching his teeth.

Jim Barnes

Remembering Hiroshima and Propaganda

By night I was sure I would hear the blast.
I had waited all the day the radio
gave the news. Solemn as a sad Gabriel,
the spokesman for the White House hailed our flag,
our boys, and then the sheer force of our will.
The language was full of high hopes: at last

we could see an end to the war, all war,
they said. I listened hard for all of us
and heard little, as the sky filled with birds.
The radio droned on and on, and now and then
a plane, too high to see, drew me to the yard
where silence rode the air as never before

when the high thin sound was gone. After sundown
I listened for a distant drumroll, looked
hard for falling stars and a glow in the east.
Nothing struck me beyond my normal world.
I would not know the force of words unleashed
by bombing Hiroshima till the decades ground

my country more insane. I am not pleased
to stand on this cliff above the Pacific,
still listening hard for the end of time,
and hear those voices speak of how well we
have it now with cobalt skies and no crime
we can't track to its source with rays of peace.

Marvin Bell

Desert Storm Troops Welcomed Back by Republicans

A shadow has come over the earth,
darker in the cities than in small towns.
The air smells yellow as after an eclipse.
There is smoke from a comet, and the burning
of books and papers taken from the blasphemous.

A smell of Middle Eastern deserts fills American nostrils.
Poetry has a new scent about it, an odor of bodies.
This happened because the acrid waste of Mexico
makes North Americans sick to the stomach.
Winds from elsewhere return the odor of our garbage.

A handfull of the furious have assembled
to protest death. They carry scythes.
They sweep the blades through the ankles of the crowd.
And the righteous sweep through the schools
looking for the unathletic, the disbelievers.

Maps of Sparta replace maps of Athens.
Blood flows at cockfights, dog fights, children's games.
Blood is poured from the bomb bays of invisible planes
onto sand miles below where it sinks in quickly.
The world is turned upside down like an hourglass.

Michael Benedikt

The Peaceable Sleepers; Or,
Poem to be Read Before, During, and After any of those
'Truly Nauseating Wars' that Truly 'Make Everybody Sick'

If only we could all see each other as we sleep, if only we could
all see how likely we all are to assume the defenseless and totally
trustful positions that even the most active body remembers best,
not by acting or reacting, but rather by relapsing; and which even
the most restless mind recalls silently, *not* by talking, but rather
by listening to those images which Peace & Quiet allow to arise,
with perfect simplicity, from the very flesh:—if only we could all
see all the closed eyes, the bowed heads, and the mouths half-
opened as if expecting, only, to be fed:—if only we could all see
all that, and the arms curved against the sides, and the hands
half-curled under, with fists and wrists relaxed, loose, and good
for fighting nothing;—if only we could all see the legs, too, poised
not for leaping straight up, at the sound of martial trumpet-calls,
for example, but rather bent at angles that would seem to preclude
not only war-like advancing, but also retreating; if only we could
all see all that, simply, and clearly—forgetting for at least some
few hours all those endless and fundamentally hostile-to-all-
humans assertions about our so-called enthusiasm for "war-
mongering": if only we could all see all this, maybe even just
once—without any of our usual slogans, speeches, and maybe even

any words at all—even just once, as a result, lifting our collective Vision beyond descriptive journalism, the nightly news, raging speechmakers on either the "Left" or the "Right," & other such relatively irrelevant preoccupations of the heirs of Walter Cronkite; if only we could all see all that—even if we didn't see it in perfectly "A.F.T."—fine-tuned-color—come to think of it, even if we didn't happen to see everybody, but maybe just a few similarly-inclined and like-minded people sleeping devotedly in the immediate neighborhood, North Side or South Side, East Side or West Side—yes, if only we could all see all that, and the wind was right, that is if conditions were favorable, that is if things were really going our way—that is, if only we could all somehow just manage even just a glimpse, even at this late date—even just a glance, perhaps, at this emphatically quiescent manifestation of our most serious human essences, preferences, and priorities . . . Why, then, we still might be able to see this world of ours afresh once again, for a change; and we might even become convinced that a human being's first dreams are somehow *still* a human's final dreams; and that all our first and final dreams are really *neither* of "Exploitation," much less of "Imperialism."

Robert Bly

For These States, 1991

This thin-lipped king with his helmeted head

Remembers the quirky fits of light

That tempt the cobra. No, the temper of the dove

Does not fit him; and nothing in the world

Can bring him to bless. He will not feed,

Nourish or help; and his rabbity hand

Lifted in the fading light of the hemlocks

Waves to them, gestures to the young to die.

Philip Booth

Places Without Names

Ilion: besieged ten years. Sung hundreds more, then
written down: how force makes corpses out of men.
Men whose spirits were, by war, undone: Salamis,

Shiloh, Crécy. Lives going places gone, Placenames
now, no faces. Sheepmen sent to Passchendaele:
ever after, none could sleep. Barely thirty years:

sons like fathers gone back to the Marne. Gone again to
Argonne Forest, where fathers they could not remember
blew the enemy apart, until they got themselves

dismembered. Sons, too, shot. Bull Run, Malvern Hill:
history tests. Boys who knew left foot from right
never made the grade. No rolls kept. Voices lost,

names on wooden crosses gone to rot. Abroad,
in rivers hard to say, men in living memory
bled their lives out, bodies bloating far downstream.

On Corregidor, an island rock of fortress caves,
tall men surrendered to small men: to each other
none could speak. Lake Ladoga, the Barents Sea, and Attu:

places millhands froze, for hours before they died.
To islands where men burned, papers gave black headlines:
Guadalcanal. Rabaul. Saipan. Iwo. Over which

men like torpedoes flew their lives down into the Pacific.
Tidal beaches. Mountain passes. Holy buildings
older than this country. Cities. Jungle riverbends.

Sealanes old as seawinds. Old villages where,
in some foreign language, country boys got laid.
Around the time the bands again start up, memory

shuts down, each patriot tho prisonei uf hls own tlag.
What gene demands old men command young men to die:
The young gone singing to Antietam, Aachen, Anzio.

To Bangladore, the Choisin Reservoir, Dien Bien Phu,
My Lai. Places in the heads of men who have no
mind left. Our fragile idiocy: inflamed five times

a century to take up crossbows, horsepower, warships,
planes, and rocketry. What matter what the weapons,
the dead could not care less. Beyond the homebound wounded

only women, sleepless women, know the holy names:
bed-names, church-names, placenames buried in their
sons' or lovers' heads. Stones without voices,

save the incised name. Poppies, stars, and crosses:
the poverty of history. A wealth of lives. Ours, always
ours: these holy names, these sacrilegious places.

Michael Dennis Browne

Gulf War Dream

my legless son arriving home from school,
demanding to know what's on TV, which cartoons,
rings under his eyes, his seven-year-old
face pitiless: *what's on? what's on?*

first, I say, *first, before TV, tell me*
how you are, give me a hug, did this
happen to you in school today? tell me,
who did this to you? look at me.

he doesn't want to talk about it,
doesn't want to look, to touch, it seems
the wounds are old, it seems he gets by
quite nicely on his hands,

and pushing past me toward the TV,
white-faced, raging: *what's on? what's on?*

Amy Clampitt

The War Memorial

The rain-god Tlaloc, hungering for blood,
the war-god, hummingbird-gartered
Huitzilopochtli, the drugged booty

of a huger, cleverer hunger, stir
in a museum hall of nightmare, where
Asshur the bellicose and Marduk, who

rode forth to set the world in order,
are neighbors, where the drifts and dunes
of long immobilized cuneiform begin

to move again, a bas-relief of dread
like the long scar, the black cicatrice
of memory not yet embalmed but raw,

those drifts of origami at its foot:
to trace whose length is to reopen
what George Fox, compelled at Lichfield

to take off his shoes, walked barefoot
in—the channel of the blood of those
who fell. For what? Can someone tell us?

Jane Cooper

Fragments

Fragments of the established world
flame and submerge, they tear away. Day by day
we witness fresh catastrophes   Strange
how most people see nothing, most people
feel the earth firm under their feet when it is
flaming

E. S. Reeve

> "You know, politics has been very good
> for us as a family." — Barbara Bush

"You know,
politics has been very good
for us as a family."

— Barbara Bush

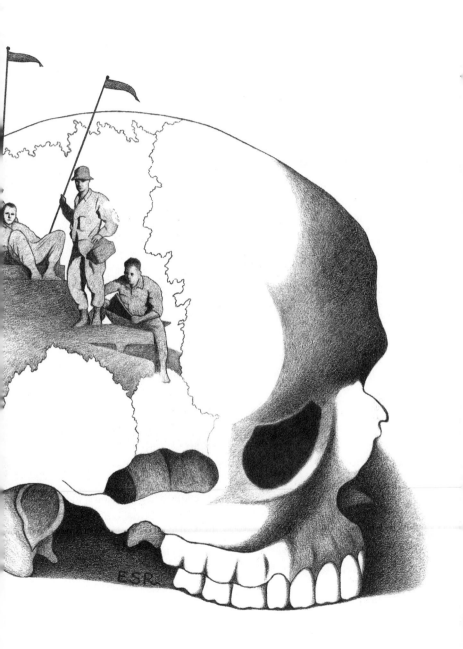

Jayne Cortez

Global Inequalities

Chairperson of the board
is not digging for roots
          in the shadows
There's no dying of hunger-stare
          in the eyes of
          Chief executive officer of petroleum
Somebody else is sinking into
          spring freeze of the soil
Somebody else is evaporating in
          dry wind of the famine
     There's no severe drought
          in mouth
of Senior vice president of funding services
     No military contractor is sitting
          in heat of a disappearing lake
No river is drying up in kidneys of
          a minister of defense
Under-secretary of interior is not writing
          distress signals on shit house walls
Do you see a refugee camp cooped up in head of
          Vice president of municipal bonds
There's no food shortage in belly of
          a minister of agriculture
Chief economic advisors are
               addicted to diet pills
Banking committee members are
               suffering from obesity
Somebody else is sucking on dehydrated nipples
Somebody else is filling up on fly specks

The Bishops
are not forcing themselves to eat bark
The security exchange commission members
are sick from
too many chocolate chip cookies
The treasury secretary
is not going around in circles
looking for grain
There's no desert growing in nose of
Supreme commander of justice
It's somebody else without weight
without blood without land
without a cloud cover of water on the face
It's somebody else
Always somebody else

Philip Dacey

The Neighbors

"Ask yourself who you would prefer as a
neighbor—Saddam Hussein or George Bush."
—Mary Jane Laub
Christian Science Monitor, Feb. 25, 1991

I walk out my front door
to enjoy the summer evening,
the silk hand of the breeze
immediately eastward,
Saddam is watering his lawn.
He sees me and waves absentmindedly,
absorbed in the sound of the drops slapping against grass.
On the west side, George reclines
in a lounge chair, a newspaper folded on his lap
as he looks at nothing in particular,
a car passing, a bird hopping at a distance.

They're good neighbors.
It's true I worried when they moved in,
one right after the other.
I had heard stories.
And there I was between them.
But I have seen them pass each other on the street
with an acknowledging nod
and even sometimes chat for a while
before they part with smiles and touches
on the arm, the back.
From time to time I borrow things, too,

a ladder from Saddam, a drill from George.
As I said, they're good neighbors.

Only occasionally
a small hand pushes up
from the ground their lots enclose,
breaking the level green,
the fingers uncurling
toward the light
and moving with an appearance
of great expressiveness,
and then only briefly
before a small engine starts up
and low blades
whirr quietly, restoring
the uninterrupted expanse
of the neighborhood
we take such pride and pleasure in
on summer evenings
like this one.

Diana Der-Hovanessian

At Mt. Auburn Cemetery

"Defense Secretary Weinberger fears acknowledging genocide
by Turks will offend them."

My father is lying in a green
field, green, green under a sun
so hot the yellow wheat and pale
straw have turned green in his eyes.
He closes them. He is fifteen.
The green field is Armenia.
The sun is the Armenian sun
of 1915. He closes his eyes
and seventy years have passed.
I am lying in a green field
in Massachusetts under a sun
so hot it has turned the yellow
weeds green inside my eyes.
I close them tighter and the entire
field turns red. I touch it
with blind fingers. It is not wet
with either blood or tears
like his fields. "Hairig,"
I say, "I am so sorry.
What can I do? How can I talk to you
when this soil that gave you haven
and home with its government
says you never existed.
What can I say, I who therefore
cannot be here to say it?"

Stephen Dunn

After Desert Storm

It's true that victory, righteously pursued
and won, is as heady as good sex with someone
you thought loved someone else. But the night
is cold when the sweat dries, even colder
when the phone rings and it's him,
who could be you in the interchangeable dark.
The parades are about to begin, and let them.
There was only a small mendacity in the joy
you felt when she leaned toward you, and isn't
any joy rare enough to deserve its day?
The corpses are everywhere.
Pleasure should be more pleasurable than this.

Clayton Eshleman

Mortified Citizen

What *does* the soul want, Jim Hillman?
Does it want to intercede between us and
these Kuwait Morgue mutilated faces,
to stitch "the knowledge of the beauty of death"
into us, so that such a suture
becomes a sutra throughout us?

Then the Iraqis split the woman's head in 3,
dumped her at her father's feet.

The soul's grief is
it persuades no one. On the ancient scales,
it underweighs a feather. Here,
the window of imagination is always
blood-spattered. I see through the blood.
I see, through the blood.
"I see through." —The Blood.

   (as they collected
the chopped-off cocks from the battlefield,
others appeared in the clouds,
chopped-off foetal cocks
in cloud bellies shredding by)

Bush, said to be most present,
now intensifying his invisibility,
has just urged me to leave the sphere of
    the positively given,
and to take up negativity as the historical
    course of man.

Bush, who took my hand when I was tiny,
now closing me, like an account,
has just explained that upon his ascension,
the tabulability of things actually ended.
As compensation, he has painted my eyes with
  secularity, hung
  zeros from my lips.

Never to forget
that by thrusting urns of blazing semen into the female
  dark, the Husseins & Bushes
have blackened the walls of nature
and, into BC   AD, split the human heart,
    2 warring outposts,
    4 earthen arms, without bodies,
    around a pit, attempting
    across zero
    to embrace?

David Ferry

Nature Poem

The gulf drinks air, fire, oil, and lamentation.

The surface of the water winks and glitters,

sparkling with a thousand points of light.

Roland Flint

Seasonal

The last freezing rain of winter
or the first bona fide spring rain
pittering its intermittent music
on the roof and copper gutters
is what you wake to a few days
after the killing has almost
stopped, in the gulf. It is a sound
filled with cleansing new shingles,
wet and black, with crocuses,
and, just behind them, forsythia,
tulips, azaleas, spring. But it doesn't
wash away last night's news, one
hundred and fifty thousand Iraqis died,
mostly from our bombing: not
the Elite Guards, but less loyal
Muslims, Kurds, and Christian Assyrians,
driven out to and trapped on
the front lines of policies
for which they did not elect
to die, these weeks black rain fell
down, in the light or dark, day in,
night out, a bloody, percussive
anthem to our great victory over
Hussein and the inhuman poor.
Now, while the lisping patter
genially wakens our house in
a birdsung Maryland suburb,
in Baghdad a season of wind and heat,
of cholera and typhus begins.

Reginald Gibbons

Poetry after the Recent War

> *After an idea, a tactic, an ambiguous*
> *renunciation, of César Vallejo*
>
> *For Sterling Plumpp*

Blown to a tatter by wine, the cry of one gull or mew of one
    cat sounds nearly the same as a fleeing child's cry near
    dark.
Should I try to refine the paced unfolding of my syntax?

The appointed and the elected yawn after eating, they travel to
    games and medical examinations in bombers, but in public
    they condescend, shuddering with a repressed paroxysm of
    triumph.
Should I rework an unsatisfying rhythm?

The president of the nation lied about everything and hid
    his crimes and was elected and then withholding his plans
    from all but his most trusted parasites he rushed to war.
After that, devote a year to a poem in Chinese stanzas?

The excitement of the elected as death approaches swells and
    swells like pus in a boil; and the citizens wait and
    trust.
Should I control more carefully the scope of my allusions?

The generals calculate a future count of skulls.
Should I confer with my colleagues about the analysis
    of discourse?

Revolutionaries and revolutionary poets argue in a secret
    meeting about who is friend and who is enemy, and the
    enemies of even those who are right to rebel must die.
Should I reconsider my punctuation?

In the recent war, before the soldiers were sent into
    combat, they were ordered to dig fifty thousand graves in
    the sand.
After news of that, should I elaborate a simile?

When the war was on, the fifty thousand graves proved to be an
    unnecessary scruple.
Thinking back about them buried in their trenches, should I
    change the narrative voice in my poems?

The war roared far away like a furnace whose white flame feeds
    on dark straw.
Should I count out syllables and stresses?

My countrymen were dropping bombs on people, and on the place
    where writing was invented and where the first poem, a
    prayer to a now dead goddess of harvest, was written down.
Shall I consider whether I am more in the print or more in the
    oral tradition?

"This company is a lethal weapon," Capt. Larnell Exum,
    commander of Company A, said proudly as his men prepared
    to board their helicopter. "We're going to deal some
    death. And this is what we're fighting for," he added,
    whipping a pair of women's black silk underwear from
    inside his helmet.
Should I try to make less use of symbols?

The television fanfared with timpani and trumpets the solemn
    exciting entertainment of the deaths that had been
    scheduled for the evening news.
After that, should I spend a while searching for a rhyme?

To object to death brings accusals by righteous love-of-death
    and attacks by smiling love-of-death.
At such a moment, I should study the variations of the myths
    of Zeus and Coyote and Staggerlee?

Compassionless brutalized sons are mobbing the excited streets
    to try to give birth to a giant father who will love and
    kill them.
Should I sincerely invoke a muse?

"This is the headquarters of my counterpart," the general
    said, and the press corps laughed, then the videotaped
    image of an apartment building in a bombsight turned to
    outflung dust and fell and disappeared.
Should I perfect the delicacy of poetic closure?

"Like shooting fish in a barrel," "like a turkey-shoot,"
    "like a video arcade," "like roaches when you turn on the
    light," four pilots said to television reporters after
    climbing out of their planes.
Should I ponder the master tropes of metaphor and metonymy?

There are toy soldiers because soldiers are the toys of power.
Should I rank my words on my page like a phalanx of purified
    diction?

There are museums constructed like castles and mansions
    because art is so often the trophy of wealth.
Therefore shall I recite my poems under bridges and in the
    catatonic corners of soup kitchens?

And anyway, a lynching is going by with a man on its shoulder.
Should I spend a half-hour on a problematical stanza?

Ancient lost goddesses of grace are weeping with grief
    far away in the place where they were banished.
Shall I posit an aesthetic experience?

Mothers who taught their sons peekaboo two decades ago are
    weeping with grief, thrown to the ground by news of
    irrevocable death.
Should I analyze the linguistic components of infant babble?

Fathers who smoothed the foreheads of fevered young daughters
    are shaking with grief as unappeasable death shrieks in
    their ears.
Shall I outline the elements of poetry?

Men and women who lay limb to limb with women and men and men
    and women they loved are neither men nor women now with the
    inhuman moaning that grief pushes out of their mouths.
Shall I say to the rose, "Thou art sick"?

The many dead who lie torn and akimbo like dolls silently
    scream and scream; those hurt but still living, looking
    at the television pictures of the dead lying torn and
    and akimbo like dolls, watch and are silent.
Shall I frame in anthropological terms why the objections to
    war are so few and do not prevail?

The church on this side of the war holds sacred two crossed
    pieces of wood stained with blood—a simple instrument of
    torture that might as well be a spear or a gun.
Shall I compile the meanings of the allegorical lily?

What used to be real is pale and what is unreal—like a
    sporting event or ice inside the skull or the crazed
    frenzy of climactic explosions—becomes all real.
Shall I invent a riddling rattle inside the doll-belly of
    a poem?

Allen Ginsberg

After the Big Parade

Millions of people cheering and waving flags for joy in Manhattan

Yesterday've returned to their jobs and arthritis now Tuesday—

What made them want so much passion at last, such mutual delight

Will they ever regain these hours of confetti'd ecstasy again?

Have they forgotten that Corridors of Death gave such victory?

Will 200 thousand more desert deaths across the world be the cause

for the next rejoicing.

Diane Glancy

America

What a place
all the swell guns the tomahawks
stepping your big foot in where
Geronimo wouldn't.

Great America
all right
so you did it
you made party favors and confetti
of the land
yo sorties
yo bunkers
what those helicopters called
the fast ones
you know that come in off the boats
out there in the Gulf?

Put it down then
get right in with all your feet
light of nations
blow-torch of the world.

Patricia Goedicke

Whenever She Speaks Up

Frieda, one of Gulliver's little known Brobdignagian mistresses,
wakes up to find herself tied down, trussed to the pavement like some
big beautiful dirigible in the middle of a crowded intersection
just outside Washington, D.C.

Gulliver, why have you forsaken her? Cars drive
their black tires over her thighs.
Democracy indeed! And the nights are worse.
Cockroaches, half finished ideas
climb all over her body.

Meanwhile, in the Halls of Justice,
one or two ex-fighter pilots and a few nervously
dithering basketball players are sending her kids off to war.
What if she grabbed up a handful of gunboats
and waded the glorious Potomac after them?

Whenever she speaks up, instantly
they rape her down.
Some of them just want to crawl back where they come from
with gun and camera, occupy her womb.
How can she help but bleed over them, massive rivers of arrogant
fraternity brothers murdering other people's children?

Crazed legislators like mosquitoes, midget cars run amok
scourge all but the money makers from the Rotunda.
In the stale, black rubber smell of overload
sweat stands up on her neck like tumors, her brain refuses to lie down.

Short circuited, she keeps waiting for thunderbolts, some long ago lost
electrical connection. What could the Author have been thinking of,
turning so many of his offspring against each other?
She wonders why she ever paid any attention to Him in the first place:
Him with his little stick.

Now, remembering the nursery, the video games and the toy golf
        clubs,
the 28 flavors of ice cream she fed him whenever he asked,
Frieda picks up Gulliver from the sidewalk, she pinches him
        with her thumb.
She can't *stand* him; she says she would rather suffocate
in her own vomit that have anything more to do with him.
But he is her son.

Albert Goldbarth

Section Three

What's amazing isn't the war,
of course: the war has always been with us.
In Doré's engraving of Abel and Cain
the murdering brother stands in a pose we know
by now, the death-lust half burnt out of him
and still half-stiffening him in adrenaline readiness
—the other brother, centered in Doré's theatrical light,
is simply empty now of everything. And
on the ground, a muscular writhe of root
or cloth or fallen branch—something bunched
and darkened, to alleviate the undetailed middle plane—
is reminiscent of the serpent, yes, as if it
lashed its way here from the Garden, from that leafy, dim
pre-Neolithic haven, just to witness this and
make sure its mission would be carried on.
Pages later: "Joshua Committing the Town of Ai
to the Flames: and "The Slaying of the Midianites"
and . . . more, too much more, so much blood
that it becomes the medium of theme
the way the ink becomes the medium of place and person.
Bosch will show us these cruelties as well, and Goya.
It isn't a secret. The movies know it. Every
front-page photograph of bodies in Iraq
has been developed in a bath
of acid squeezed straight out of the rocks
on the slopes around Eden or Olduvai.
We've dreamed the poses of this dying
for a million years, and there they are again
at breakfast and then in the afternoon edition.

It's tragic, oh certainly tragic, and yet
as common as rust, a human rust, a walk
to buy the paper through the old corrosive air.

What's truly amazing is section three
—the newly-engaged are beaming out, unmarked
by anything other than promise; light's completion
seems to come in merely officiating over these smiles.
Just a page more, and the married are routinely making babies,
and the quilt fair, and the boat show, and the jello-wrestling contest
are announced. Who *are* they, going about their business
                in "Business,"
"Neighbors," "Entertainment"? Lollygaggers who have yet
                to catch up
with the pellmell armada of grief? or supramystics, who
have folded their torsos lotuswise, serenely closed their eyes, and
levitated above it all, as if on invisible garage-bay lifts? Are these
the loathsome?—the insufferably greedy, the complacent,
the morally blind, the ones whose small but daily fortune is a stink
inside the overriding aromas of human misery. Or are these
the blessed?—these, the next stage, here
already; these, the ones the planet was intended to accommodate
the first time, on the ur-green primocontinent, but something went
awry, and now they're here, again, in blurs of easeful waving
at the curbside. Aren't these lives unreal, leaking
of mirage-steam or of fogged narcotic landscape? Yes,
no, aren't these the fully-bodied dream-lives
we fight *for*, and would defend against bedevilment?
On any day, the questions spin
like a color wheel out of 5th grade science, until they make
a blankness we could funnel into. My friends are
writing their poems about daffodil country, writing
about some shattered hypodermics in the hall.
"Right now I'm working on a poem about oxymorons,"
she tells me, "you know: *jumbo shrimp* or when Thoreau writes
28 lbs. soft hardbread. Or THIS is amazing," she
unfolds today's paper. ACCIDENT (then, smaller type:)
Allies Die By Friendly Fire.

Donald Hall

The Coalition

If among earth's kings Lord Gilgamesh should remain unreasonable,
if civility refuses to assume citizenship between the rivers,
Sir Agamemnon will assemble a diligent Protestant coalition

to administer death as appropriate lesson and punishment.
We'll station right-thinking King Herod with his updated hoplites
backed by Xin the Emperor's deathless terracotta battalions

beside Mercury, Mars, and Athena from the province of Olympus
to institute, as a deterrent, termination with extreme prejudice.
Young Colonel Bonaparte, upgrading to Alexander, will distribute

slaughter by African blowguns, phalanxes, tortoises from Cipango,
hairy helicopters from Attila's stables, Cyclopean missiles,
and Greek fire to melt brute Saracens flourishing scimitars.

If Lord Gilgamesh should remain unreasonable, we will coalesce
to incinerate retreating Uruki soldiers, furthering the project
of Pharoah Death, Imperator Death, Shogun Death, President Death.

Sam Hamill

Yellow Ribbons, Madness, and Victory

While the nation welcomes home its heroes,
two hundred thousand corpses burn
and rot in the desert under billowing clouds
of oil smoke and mountains of rubble.
A pale moon at vernal equinox.
Wet snow falls on blossoming daffodils.

Linda M. Hasselstrom

Thanksgiving Prayer

Behind me, the black shadow of a church
reaches out from every height in Scotland.
Through chaotic centuries, their stone hymns
drown screams, the whine of sword blades.
Conflicting legends paint their floors
with the thick, red blood of martyrs;
smoke from human flesh sketches
separate creeds against blue sky.
From their aisles blows a chill Christian wind
driving men and women to their knees
in the blood of their own ancestors,
their own children.

Surrounded by ancient churches—
with the opulent liquor of entreaty, hymns
and Christian sanctity oozing from their stones—
I pray on the beach.
Empty my pockets of stones
and shells from the stormy coasts,
place them in a circle around sage from home.
Earth lies quiet under my feet; air sweeps past
in storm clouds; rain runs down my face;
warmth from my heart and fingers
stands for the fourth element, fire.

The salt stings my throat, scorched raw
by years of bawling adoration
into empty stone vaults and naves,
of begging stone-eared saints
to turn their sleek smiles on me.
My eyes burn with tears
for love I'll never know again.
Sharp-tongued Cuillin Hills chant ferocious love
from heather heights to lakes filled with tears.
Today he walked beside me.
Inside his coat, I crawled down the tunnel
to the burial crypt.
I did not lie down.
Now I stand facing sea wind.
White foam sweeps away the lighter stones,
the sagebrush and tobacco.
I ask only to come back here;
salt spray eases the pain in my throat.
The hand inside my pocket clutches heather
dug between the standing stones.
When I get home, I will plant it
on my husband's grave.

William Heyen

The Truth

Across Brockport Village, a blight of orange & yellow ribbons
meant to remember our half-million participants
in "Operation Desert Storm," those who put their lives on line
to protect our country, as our president says.
Darkening ribbons encircle trees, telephone poles,
mailboxes, porch rails—so I was understandably half bored
& half nuts with war & ugliness, so climbed to my roof
& tied a large black configuration of bow & ribbons
to my aerial. Up there, I saw how it divides the winter sky
with its alphabet of one emotional letter, a vowel. . . .

At first, no one noticed, but then a car turned around.
Later, a police cruiser slowed down, & then another.
A reporter stopped for that infamous photo that appeared in *Time*
& the first of a hundred interviews I declined,
& neighbors gathered. My phone kept ringing off the wall,
people yelling "bastard," & "traitor," & "get it the hell down,
or else." . . . Eventually, my best friend came to my door
& asked me why. I explained, "I can't explain." Others followed,
& insisted. "No comment," I said. "I don't want trouble,"
I said. "Read Hawthorne's 'The Minister's Black Veil.'"

I still like the way the black bow & ribbons flutter,
stark but suggestive of comic dark, serious, direct,
my own American allegiance & patriotic light.
Parson Hooper had his reasons, & half understood them,
but when he slept or spoke, his breath trembled the veil,
& even holy scripture seemed filtered by the terrible
transformation of black crepe into symbol. In the end,
not even his creator could commend the visionary parson
who espied the truth that separates & condemns.
Above my village, this beauty of black bow & ribbons.

Jonathan Holden

Gulf: January 17, 1991

> Ah, love, let us be true
> To one another!
> —Matthew Arnold

(for Ana)

And didn't our love seem almost a political act,
to turn away from the footage of the F-15s
following each other in single file
along a slow assembly-line as if on parade,
toy after toy, each copy being lifted, smoking
off the scorched belt, then the next
and the next being mass-produced into an industrial sky.
As we kissed, and kissed more deeply, trying
to make the picture go away, to deny this, I saw
that what we had been watching, what so fascinated us
was only another kind of factory, that it was inevitable
the activity we call "war" be conducted in round-the-clock shifts,
that military bases and state penitentiaries
are designed to manufacture identical deaths
as heartlessly as a commercial egg factory
where the lights are kept on to get the hens
to produce eggs faster than is natural. The men
all in the same sand-and-spinach uniform
were as similar as hens. Even the General strutting

like a fat rooster had donned those funny pajamas
like a surgeon's gown, a carpenter's apron—
what boys wear when they put on
the frightening costumes of efficiency,
roll up their sleeves and get ready to get down
to business, to be men. Wasn't it Spengler
who said it takes about twenty years for hens to forget,
for a generation to be bred ignorant of the shop floor,
enough time for new men who,
because they don't know any better, are willing
to put on the killing pajamas, the aprons again
and, like their grandfathers, earnestly go to work?
Isn't it twenty years since I used to watch, rapt,
with field glasses, the fleas circling
the hive of Alameda Naval Air Station,
the carrier like a slate, shelved landform
that would appear overnight, a grey grandmother,
to babysit the skyline for a week,
then go back to work in Asia. Ah, love,
didn't it seem subversive to turn off the t.v.,
how we followed each other wordless, deep
into the immediate truth of the next kiss.
And the next. And decided then and there
we would take our costumes off for the afternoon,
we would not go to work that day
or the next. Or the next.

Bill Holm

Watching the War on the Oregon Coast

I

I press the remote knob; electricity made visible snaps to attention, colored dots arrange themselves into the old pilot's crew cut head—broad shoulders, square chin, a correct blue blazer and shirt. "It's Super Bowl for three young pilots," he says. "They're all excited to show their stuff." The dots flicker and re-order themselves into a garish night sky over an electric city. It's a video game sky, boxed, with a hand lever that moves the stars into position. Flashes dart, counter flashes chase them, little puffs of light in the blue dark. See Patriot find Scud! It's a perfectly executed play! Those tall apartment buildings are electric goal posts! "It's a Fourth of July sky," says the old pilot's head with mounting fervor. "Just look at that accuracy!" The image flickers: gray boxes with X's at the center. A computer dot whizzes down, pops the X. "See! See the inside of that building implode! A direct hit!" Somewhere in the universe, bells ring, the free game sign lights up, drinks on the house.

II

Outside, on the Oregon coast, the winter tide rumbles, throwing up wet logs the size of bombs, banging them against the stone cliffs. Noisier than T.V. out there. . . The stars flicker; one tries a shot at another but misses, fizzles

out in the sea, toward Japan. The crab boat lights a few
miles off shore are steady and even, their drag nets combing
the bottom for meat. Under the sea, the trapped crabs march
backwards, mouth filaments wavering like radar, claws
snapping and clacking at the line, at each other, at water, at
air, at nothing. Closer in, the mussels clamp onto the shore
rocks tight, close their mouths, not giving out name, rank, or
serial number. The anemone opens its tentacles like an
evangelist's fingers, beckoning believers into the altar of the
stomach.

III

If the sea had had an industrial revolution, who would it
bomb by night? Would the bombs open in the center,
beautiful as roses, as ours do? Would it all happen in calm
silence, on television, as it does with us? Or would the sea
leave it to the crabs, with their bad tempers and sweet meat,
the crabs swelled up to the size of airplanes, spreading their
claws like red bony wings.

Edwin Honig

The Old New War

Backed into barren winter
I think of plenty stored
inside abandoned houses
near the shore
that loll on stilts
barnacled and silvery green
imagining the appetite
of absent hurricanes
come sniffing in
to batter and consume.

The sloping Stone Age boulder
ocean-liner size
opening on the road behind
invites lost histories
back to loggers driving sleds
down some erased
now heavily snowed-in trail.

Do lions beg permission
of their prey?

Some natives still do
who kill to eat.

Let the lioness protect her pride
against the hungry lion
till trophy hunters avid
for pride and prey
slide in.

Even in drastic beginnings
there's time to play the cub
watching a slaughter of the innocents
in shady camouflage
paradisal to any being
living for the day.

Lives needing not to know
inside from out
drive into a sudden emptiness
where turkey buzzards
circling over prey to come
with springtime calving
trace in airy patterns
childhood's dream
of stingless gliding.

Colette Inez

The Dance of Daemons

(for Miriam Beerman)

1.

Bodies fall in a dream of thumbscrews and prods,
scourges and nails. Christ on a revolving cross
twitches with lights. On the steps of the cathedral,
a childless crone prays for her womb to open its door.
Numb with cold, children count filched coins,
call her Mother of Dreams.

She will bury a talisman to pull out of earth
when God leans down from a green cloud
to give her another body not like a dog's hind leg,
a camel's back, a gibbous moon.

In the marriage of the crazed and the poor,
the moon in its caldron of sky
gives birth to an astonishment:
the venerable Sarah at last is with child.
Let the owl-headed angel astride a black wolf
fly to the barren lands of no hope.

2.

Head shaved—it was rumored her hair
concealed demons—a bride is flung into a well
on her wedding night. Her groom claims

she is of the Devil's Brood.
Townspeople are hardened to her cry:
"I am the Rose of Sharon, a Lily of the Valleys."
Because we remember her, curse her accuser,
she will not fall mute with her store of songs.

3.

In war rooms the dead are divorced
from their tears, chosen for heaven or hell
by an officer partial to dogs.
In the underworld, his Dobermans will snarl
at the golden bough of Aeneas
under the rule of Baal.

The Commandant, at one with his beasts,
is pacified by music. Blood on his jowls drips
to the tick of commandeered watches
on a shelf of spectacle frames, dentures,
brooches, pins, wedding rings and tattooed skin.
How shall he conjure the Devil?
Invocations from a grimoire: ". . . come forth
instantly or I shall torture you endlessly."

4.

In the gray smoke of the camps, through the gate,
the hapless stumble in a dream. Their souls are bestirred
to have pity on the world. They illumine as they burn
like candles of tallow. Their bones will mix
with the semen of beasts, the exhalation of clouds
fused with air.

One man tills the land, the other complains.
If God lived on earth, his house would be stoned.
If the mule had horns, none would call him stubborn.
To sow memories is to reap a lost world.
What shall the angels record?
What runes shall we say to safeguard the names?
Rachel, Sucha, Lebel, Dov, Cingany, Barbu, Zingaro,
Rom, Stanislaw, Magdalene, Mustafa, Fatima, Abdul,
Wanda, Yuri, Lem.

Bodies fall in a rain of tombs under lindens
and palms, under the bough of the hazel
that will bear fruit at Lammastide.
Roses and skulls float in water
which feeds the grass. Angel, bird, naked worm,
swallowed by our creation. We are captives,
at the last, to the darkness of matter.

5.

Therefore damn Lucifer and the Dogs of Hell,
the cat in the guise of the Devil, the asp,
the basilisk spawned by a cock and a toad,
the lizard bringing messages from realms of the dead,
O Oualbpaga O Kammara O Kamalo O Karhennon O Amagaaa!
Transmogrified names of sun god Osiris
and Set, Patriarch of death.

And cast the spell of Ninevah:
"He who forges the image, he who enchants—
the spiteful face, the evil eye,
the mischievous mouth, tongue . . . lips, words.
Spirits of the sky, remember!

Dale Jacobson

Night Vision of the Gulf War

1

They came to rearrange the dust and shadows.
They were right because it felt good.
They released the power of seven
Hiroshima bombs, 88,500 tons,
to alter the attitude of bridges
modify the roads and their vistas,
amend the attitude of buildings. . . .

Some 200,000 buried alive—no one
cared to keep count, or could.
Through the billowing smoke, the clouds of earth,
the light from the flames shifted,
the shadows shifted and the dust.
Everything shifted.

2.

In the capital of the empire the trees
dormant in their winter sturdiness
waited in their branches for their green
elaboration toward the sky.

If the stars were the nation's pity
they would be dark and hard
like the dense core of the gold ball

the Commander-in-Chief, "the Great Ass-Kicker,"
shot around the green while
on the desert the soldiers died.

It was a festival of death, yellow ribbons
everywhere, the color of pale distance by moonlight,
or the water-logged blade of a fallen windmill—
or the color of poison—easy hatred, easy love,
the sentimental crime: the citizens, so angry lost or afraid
in their own country, they revelled in bombing another—
power in their name, though they themselves had none.

The million-dollar missiles rose over the sea,
and the swift jets. The pilots said:
"We own the night."

   3.

More likely the night now owns us . . .

It is a country larger than the nation,
more ancient than history,
and flies no flag.

In Iraq the night is owned by the corrupted water.

It rises like a poisonous mist around the Iraqi children,
hurries them away—55,000—
perhaps another 170,000 within the year.

The night belongs to the rising and falling of the wind,
its additions and subtractions
through which their deaths move, unnoticed.

No stealth bomber is as stealthy as the night
that comes home.

4.

Near Fort Ransom, North Dakota
is perhaps the oldest pyramid in the world.

No one knows who built it.

The Fort is long gone.

The rains that fall on the absent Fort,
and on the pyramid, arrive
out of the horizon where the waters climb
tiny ladders and everything is flat.

The droplets spin through
the immense shadow of the clouds.

J. Kates

English as a Foreign Language

The teacher writes *war*.
One pupil, finding it hard
to say the letter "r,"
accidentally asks, *why?*
One of the orphans starts to cry.
This, the teacher thinks, is more
than I bargained for.

Forging a new language
is the first campaign.
Those who have learned
catch as catch can,
caught at a disadvantage,
need to have
the simplest things explained.

Men are no longer men,
women no longer women,
Children over *here* remain
children, while others, made
into collateral damage,
grub through rubble
or shiver in the dark, afraid.

The teacher writes, *war*.
A pupil well on her way
(but not yet *there*)
accidently asks, *where?*
The orphans all keep quiet.
This, the teacher thinks,
is more like it.

Edward Kleinschmidt

Continuum

The time we've had having time. Alongside the boneyard
We take a hard right. We have never been wrong before,
Vertebra or not vertebra, walking through slush
Of centuries, always towards the center of something
That has caused us to concentrate on it, the center
Of the continent, perhaps. We haven't said this
Before so if we say this again we can say we've said
This before. That goes a long way back, goes
Inward to the place that begins lack, to the place
That spreads its emptiness like bed sheets over
Everything but beds, over the blue arm chairs we sat in
To stare into the center of fire. We have an
Anniversary of that time frequently—it's the least
We could do, in memory of each other as additional
Listeners. We read a newspaper rolled up and stuck
In a crack in the window in a room in the house: About
A man who strangled a women with her worry beads.
This makes us wonder all over again. The pain of lost
Love and lost life is the same. Ten years ago
We weren't thinking ten years later. That would have been
Vertigo of a different color. Now the wreath of
Time is simply that which is wound around.
The wound comes later now, or not at all,
Depending on who is wielding the spear. There's

A hint of air in the air. We spent the evening
Entertaining an idea. We threw a fascicle of
Wood on the fire and received a facsimile of ash
In return. We think of all the circles in a square
Box—this is a concentration technique that tenors use
to hold their high notes together. They have an ear
For hearing. They surely have a surplus of valves. The cold
Holds us together, and what else: The connection between
This time and next time, the spaces between the letters
In our names, the absence and nonsense, the sensation,
The sentence, the sentence that we continuously send each other.

Wendy Wilder Larsen

Watching

After TV war
bird tracks imprinted in snow
are bombers tracking.

David Shapiro   ►

         "Anti-War Demonstration"   ►

Denise Levertov

Misnomer

They speak of the art of war,
but the arts
draw their light from the soul's well,
and warfare
dries up the soul and draws its power
from a dark and burning wasteland.
When Leonardo
set his genius to devising
machines of destruction he was not
acting in the service of art,
he was suspending
the life of art
over an abyss,
as if one were to hold
a living child out of an airplane window
at thirty-thousand feet.

Philip Levine

"A Rabbit Snared in a Fence of Pain"

A rabbit snared in a fence of pain
screams and screams
I waken, a child again
and answer
I answer my father
hauling his stone up the last few breaths
I answer Moses bumbling before you
the cat circling three times
before she stretches out and yawns
the mole gagged on fresh leaves

In Folson, Jaroubi, alone before dawn
remembers the long legs of a boy
his own once and now his son's
Billy Ray holds my hand to his heart
in the black and white still photograph
of the exercise yard
in the long shadows of the rifle towers
we say goodbye forever
Later, at dusk the hills
across the dry riverbed
hold the last light
long after it's gone
and glow like breath

I wake
and it's not a dream
I see the long coast of the continent

writhing in sleep
this America we thought we dreamed
falling away flake by flake
into the sea
and the sea blackening and burning

I see a man curled up, the size of an egg
I see a woman hidden in a carburetor
a child reduced to one word
crushed under an airmail stamp
or a cigarette

Can the hands rebuild the rocks
can the tongue make air or water
can the blood flow back
into the twigs of the child
can the clouds take back their deaths

Thomas Lux

The People of the Other Village

hate the people of this village
and would nail our hats
to our heads for refusing in their presence to remove them
or staple our hands to our foreheads
for refusing to salute them
if we did not hurt them first: mail them packages of rats,
mix their flour at night with broken glass.
We do this, they do that.
they peel the larynx from one of our brother's throats.
We devein one of their sisters.
The quicksand pits they built were good.
Our amputation teams were better.
We trained some birds to steal their carrots.
They sent to us exploding ambassadors of peace.
They do this, we do that.
We cancelled our sheep imports.
They no longer bought our sweaters.
We mocked their greatest poet
and when that had no effect
we parodied the way they dance
which did cause pain, so they, in turn, said our God
was leprous, hairless.
We do this, they do that.
Ten thousand (10,000) years, ten thousand
(10,000) brutal, beautiful years.

Dan Masterson

Shrapnel

He is barefoot in the creek again,
wandering between his house and the next,
not fully awake from dreams of grenades
blown orange.

Clad in summer pajamas, he fondles himself
for slivers unable to rust as they rise
from the streams of his flesh: grey hairs
refusing to bend.

He enters the tunnel beneath the road
and squats there; the cannon of his voice,
reaching both flanks, commands the neighborhood
to take over.

There are no replies from the ranks;
the years have covered them with grass grown wild
in memory.

His fingers continue their search, sensing movement
within, and succeed at this left wrist
where a steel pricker stands rigid
—a miniature soldier—the point of its bayonet
piercing the skin for escape.

He draws at it with his teeth and feels it
give way; with his prisoner pinched
between finger and thumb, he crawls with the current
toward light.

Caught in the death of his squad, leaving
only the moon as a guide,
he questions his victim, frantic to learn
the invasion plans of those left behind
to drain his heart.

In the blur of morning, he watches his enemy
twist once before curling dead
in the palm of his hand.

Giving him now to the stream, using a leaf as a pallet,
he kneels to the dead man's voyage.

Cleopatra Mathis

The Small Matters of the Everyday: Two Accounts

1.

This is the story of a man.
This is guesswork from the papers,
from all of us who need to understand
a man we thought no different from ourselves.
For don't we all imagine
the tapping inside a void, a voice inside a voice
that makes more echo than sense:
Who knows what he heard
behind the normal weight of rain and wind.
Something pursued him from room to room
until he thought it was his own pulse
ticking away at each failure. He thought
he felt his heart skip, the maneuver
of a heart made wrong, a muscle
tightening like a fist around some fear
so essential it would strike to break free.

He's got his two kinds of music:
classical and country, one open, the other shut.
As brandy complements the former—the expansive talker
in any group—beer closes him down. Night after night,
he hunches over the bar, elbows out.
One morning he walks to work from the train,
seeing the perfect V of ducks
over the mirror and steel of buildings
and something in the accidental beauty of it

is intolerable. He thinks maybe it is his work
he hates. He's sick of the office, the politics
of his own geography; and even at 5 p.m. his partner
playing racquetball wonders at his vengeance,
at the batter and heft of his mean left hand.
He takes a physical cure, he takes three days and goes south
to hunt, crouching in the humming quiet of the blind
on a red fall morning. He looks into the marsh water
as he can no longer bear to look
at himself, or at this wife who escapes it all
counting stitches as she knits or kneading bread:
her hands are never still. He can no longer
bear to look at them, no longer bear the knife
buttering the bread, or the repeated mouths
chewing, body to feed the body; cannot bear
the truth of her body which he has filled
with bodies. Their faces surround him, and in this proof
of a future history, he sees nothing
but the futility of it all.
Who knows what stops him, what moves him
late one night to load a gun and move from room to room
taking the life of his wife and each child
sleeping, until it is time to turn the gun on himself.
But he never enters the last room
where the last child sleeps, or if he does, only looks
and leaves, or straightens covers,
or even kisses her in the way of any father
his sleeping child. She will wake to this story
and it will follow her all the days of her life.

2.

The other man, who keeps his old mother
and bathes his children, will bring out his wallet
for weapons in another country, for the righteous

bombs of an interpreted freedom
that will tear apart the countryside and continue
to feed the centuries' body of blood.
Violence is the fifth season this land bears,
the burning of what would lie fallow. A bomb goes off
in the middle of women shopping or shaking their rugs,
as ordinary as weather. Spring in this soil
means each particle holds the blood's chemical and trace.
Every grain of this dirt has passed through
The bones of a woman or a man.

        But money is the word, the scream
of authority, and for the sake of the living
nobody breaks terror's code, preferring to be saved
by the small matters of the everyday.
The sun is up—two violences: the daily
fire in light and the one that governs the border
twenty miles away. Still the cows chew and plod
their way over the drumlins; the children
bound for school in white stockings
wait by the lilac hedge, and the sky rains gently away
into an immaculate clearing. In the old earth,
in the silk and meal of dirt, the stalk comes pushing up.

Mekeel McBride

The Intention

We move into the field. Late summer grasses, gold
and high as our waists, open in the fragrance-soaked wind.
The man with me, a naturalist, says,
"Look. Two eagle feathers," plucks them up
then lets them float off in the brine-clean air.
Nothing of special interest to him.

He is used to finding fragments left by animals
the rest of us hardly every see. "Catch them back for me"
I say and as he places them in my hand—does this happen
because I have the audacity to love what belongs to wind?—
an eagle descends into the field awkwardly.
Thick black pool of blood congeals behind its right wing.

Shot for sport. Shot for such fierce soaring.
Shot by the hunter, earth-stranded, who weeps
in the late night whiskey-inferno
because he cannot rise above the mountains the way
that god-damned bird does easy as breathing.
I blink again. Field, gone. My sweet blond twin

who caught the warning back from wind, vanished.
The bird, still there, but skinned. As if my blinking
had pushed past external wound to see within.
Structure of what was, still visible through all the blood.
The eagle trying to use remnants of a wing
to wrap and hide the ruined body but nothing now can be

hidden. You, who so easily carried lightning back to earth
in your gold talons, will die slowly and in pain so fierce
it cannot be named. The intention to remove
everything you ever loved. Field, wind, shining
dusk, even the star-soaked dark mountain.
And that has been done.

Jay Meek

Constellations

On the way home from the classes I teach,
I ride my daughter's bike, listening
to the sprocket give its reassuring turns.
I've slung a knapsack over my shoulder
and lean into the prairie wind,
thinking of mornings like this one
when I skimmed the *Times* on microfilm—
not the news, but shadows of news.

        Under the elms, I pump and coast.
I don't know why, this summer I started
to remember a girl from my boyhood
who became a stewardess after high school.
One night, her plane blew up over Iowa
because someone on board
wanted to lift the burden of life
and took a flight full of people with him.

A week later, I sailed on the *Groote Beer*,
student ship of the Holland-America Line.
In the glass encased library this morning,
I turned through a week of shadows,
rolling them into forgetfulness
like a flock of gulls rising from a field.
A plane down over Iowa.
        Another, at Orly.

In Jerusalem, the glass booth
where Eichmann looked out upon his trial
like a game show contestant,
before they scattered his ashes
from a fishing boat outside Israeli waters.

Behind glass, trying to answer for myself,
I unwound the spool to June 4,
where I read in a list of ship sailings
we'd leave Hoboken at noon,
Pier 5, and on that night I walked the deck
remembering Marilyn Bloomquist
whose family knew ours in the old country,
while the constellations rolled
overhead toward some hardly imagined year:

nuclear domes that rise like old cathedrals,
chemical ponds, doomed farms,
space weapons that beam our wars home to us
long after everyone's gone—
what a send-up our lives are, what a fizzle.

Nelson Moe

The Snow

Tho snow was general over all of Ireland
as he dragged his sodden gabardine
through nettle fields and morning air raids.
He sought a place where he could feel
the weightlessness of things
torn clean from their leather bindings.
Rock, hill, cloud—these words
hung upon his lips like a new-found mantra.
Then the rains came, heavy like lead.
When they found him next morning
his wounds had blossomed.

James Moore

Selections from Poem-in-Progress (Section 7)

I can't help myself: I must listen. Scott Simon
sounds shaken. Perhaps, he says, we have done too much
"weapon of the week reporting," perhaps we should
(I paraphrase) have looked at what war really does.
We have already killed 20,000 people.
Why is it, he asks, we have not reported this
with the same passion as we have filed our reports
on the latest weapons systems? At its heart, the next
step is humility: to ask for the removal
of our shortcomings. Rilke: *perhaps all the dragons*
of our lives are princesses . . . only waiting to see us
once beautiful and brave. Perhaps everything
terrible is . . . something helpless that wants help from us. . . .

The amazing thing is that we all keep going.
Day two of the land war and we wait in line for movies
or socks. We watch TV and it's the same silliness
as always, not news from the War, but a comedy.
I live in a country that can fight a war
and at that same time go about business as usual.
But, really, is it any different from when we
aren't fighting a war, those "normal" days we all live
while at the same time desperation undercuts lives one by one? . . .

The shortcomings of the very idea of the normal: each moment
is its own gravestone, its own birth canal, and we keep forgetting
that, at heart, we are all poets, we are all here to note again and again
how extraordinary it is that each moment is a birth
and a death, a celebration and an injustice as terrible
as the repeated bombing of starving conscripts in bunkers.
*But when I come to touch your heart,/how shattering to find it locked /
in torrifying snow and frost! // On the fringes of my grief /
waves a parched dry handkerchief,/hoping my tears will slake its thirst.*
How strange to think of grief as an answer, rather than a problem.
That there is a thirst within us, a white flag of surrender, that only grief
assuages. How strange to think that we need to surrender to this grief.

Lisel Mueller

1990

That was the year the future arrived,
or so we thought, the promise we never gave up on.
History, the tragic figure in black,
became confused and descended on us
in a shower of gold, and we were quick to believe
the change was real, was forever, and we
were a generation elected to witness
the abolition of darkness. That year
we lived in perpetual sunshine, light
as balloons skywriting paradise.
Wasn't it the mildest winter on record,
the most benign summer? Birds flew down from the north
with dispatches of joy in their beaks.

Was it all a dream? History is back
in its funeral clothes, the shining year
behind us, a collapsed miracle,
already a legend, like childhood,
an irretrievable golden age.

Carol Muske

To the Muse

New Year's Eve, 1990

She danced topless, the light-eyed drunken girl
who got up on the bow of our pleasure boat
last summer in the pretty French Mediterranean.

Above us rose the great grey starboard flank
of an aircraft carrier. Sailors clustered
on the deck above, cheering, and caps rained down,

a storm of insignia: *S. S. Eisenhower.*
I keep seeing the girl when I tell you
the *Eisenhower*'s now in the Gulf, as if

the two are linked: the bare-breasted dancer
and a war about to be fought over oil. Caps fell
on the bow and she plucked one up, set it rakishly

on her red hair. In the introspective manner
of the very drunk, she tipped her face dreamily up,
wet her lips, an odalisque, her arms crossed akimbo

on the cap. Someone, a family member, threw a shirt
over her and she shrugged it off, laughing, palms
fluttering about her nipples. I tell you I barely knew

those people, but you, you liked the girl, you
liked the ship. You like to fuck, you told me.
The sex of politics is its intimate divisive plural,

we, us, ours. *Who's over there?* you ask—*not us.*
Your pal is there, a flier stationed on a carrier.
He drops the jet shrieking on the deck. Pitch dark:

he lowers the nose toward a floating strip of
lit ditto marks and descends. Like writing haiku—
the narrator is a landscape. A way of staying subjective

but humbling the perceiver: a pilot's view.
When you write to your friend I guess that
there are no margins, you want him to see

everything you see and so transparent is
your kind of bravado: he sees that too. Maybe
he second-guesses your own desire to soar over

the sand ruins, sit yourself in the masked pit
and rise fifteen hundred screaming feet a minute
into an inaccessible shape: falcon, hawk—Issa's

blown petals? Every headline contains haiku:
haiku contain headlines. Reinvent war, then the woman's
faithless, enslaved dance. Reinvent sailors bawling

at the rail and one intoxicated trick turning in
the dazzling light. Then the psyche re-inventing itself,
breaking the spell, reversing it. Caps on the waves, as if

they'd begun tossing away their uniforms, medals, stars.
See—I can make the girl wake up, dress, face west,
a lengthening, powerful figurehead: swept gold with fire.

I can make everything I thought indefensible change in the waves
of merciless light: the you, the me, the wars. Here is the worst
of it, stripped, humiliated—or dancing on the high deck,

bully-faced, insatiable. Here is the lie that loves us
as history personified, here's the personification: O passionate
agitatrix, swearing to you this time I can make it right.

Kathleen Norris

In Wartime

February 1991

The young Greyhound driver
heads west tonight
across North Dakota, an odd mixture
of reassurances: a childbearing Venus,
the sacred pelvis stuffed into gray
uniform pants; the strong arms and
curly crown of an Athena, but
a more motherly face; a smile that's pure
Julian of Norwich. "All will be well."

"This is Sterling Cafe," she calls out,
"Rest rooms to the left
as you go in, but the doors say 'Bucks'
and 'Does;' you never can tell
what Western humor will do.

If you don't know which you are, see me."

Near sunset we pull up at a crimson sign
that reads "Hotel." She parks the bus
and runs up the stairs to the lobby,
to an old woman in a dark blue dress.
They stand

in the gaping door
of an empty dining room,
the green light of a wall clock that reads: 6:20.

No business to contract, no passengers
to guide on or off, no packages to pick up
or deliver. "She has her walker tonight,"
one of the riders, a regular, says
to a woman on her way from Memphis
to Seattle. "She's one-hundred-and-one years old."

"An eighteen-ninety baby . . . imagine," comes the reply,
a drawl. The driver climbs back in,
the brakes sigh, and we begin to roll.

"She waits for you."
"She waits for all of us.
She says she can tell it's cold outside
when we don't stop."
The sky is the color of the sign
by now, every branch
in the line of trees west of town
is etched on this black scribble of horizon.
"She says this the the first war
she hasn't had family in."

We are heading into darkness, no need
of reading lights just now,
the highway blood-red,
shiny as a wound.
We are each of us

so fragile; born of woman,
what else could we be?
A pulse as light, as reassuring,
as rain. A breath that carries the name
of someone who loves us,
or loved us once.

Now the lights of Bismarck, twenty miles off,
the
red
heart-
beat
of the
radio towers
where I am going, where his heart still beats.
And he doesn't even know that I am coming,
my husband, in intensive care.

Sharon Olds

The Protestor

for Bob Stein

We were driving north, through the snow, you said
you'd turned 21 during Vietnam, you were
1-A. The road curved
and curved back, the branches laden, you
said you'd decided not to go
to Canada. Which meant you'd decided to
go to jail, a slender guy of
21, which meant you'd decided to be
raped rather than to kill, if it was their
life or your ass, it was your ass.
We drove in silence, such soft snow
so heavy borne-down. That was how I'd come to
know I loved America—
when the men had to leave, they could never come back,
I looked and loved every American
needle on every American tree,
my soul was in it. But if I were taken and
used, taken and used, I think
my soul would die, I think I'd be easily broken,
the work of my life over. And you'd said
This is the world of my life, to say with my
body itself You fuckers you cannot
tell me who to kill. As if there were a

spirit free of the body, safe from it.
After a while you talked about your family,
not starting, as I had, with
husband and children, leaving everyone else out—
you started with your grandparents
and worked your way back, away from yourself,
deeper and deeper into Europe, the Torah
buried sometimes in the garden, sometimes
swallowed and carried in the ark of the body itself.

Walter Pavlich

Late at Night, in the Bathroom, the Secretary of State

It is easy to imagine the Secretary
of State brushing his teeth, shaving

little blood-dots onto the flannel collar
of his pajamas. He soothes each eye-

brow with a wipe of a dry finger,
closes the door to make a sound

unromantic yet controlled. He's con-
sidering milk toast to feed his ulcer,

and an Astaire/Eleanor Powell movie
on UHF 36, a distant station his TV

can barely hold onto. Astaire taps
away (while the Secretary sleeps in

a chair), sings "I've Got My Eyes On You."
A wobble away of the earth, the sun

shines its klieg light on villages
while Eleanor and Fred go out for coffee

as the world prepares its roll-call,
open unmusical auditions for death.

Molly Peacock

Baubles after Bombs

Little metal symbols gambol in the bright
pastures of the cases—the world in sight
for a moment, coincidences hinged
together in a genuine plan, parts phalanged
as finger joints, clasped and ringed
in the jewelry display. Elsewhere someone's job
is picking arms and fingers from the rubble,
while we pick out our pins, one a cat's head—
it doesn't look severed at all. Meant to be
displayed with turquoise eyes that do not sob,
chin a perfect end to its body . . . Rubble
searching for human debris is all our job, bent
on recovering as we are, so in this case we see
our hopes made gold facts. Beauty in a world sacked
is whimsy's rearrangement of organs and limbs,
all things in miniature akin: a frog's head,
a dog's head, gemmed hearts, chained to a pin.

F. D. Reeve

The Silence of War

If a man's dead,
do guns or bombs
or missiles opening his cellar door
make any noise?

From the house you live in
can you hear Semiramis
in her garden climbing the marble stairs
to her gold throne?

Mystics who pray
for peace in our time
feel the wind on the floor and whisper,
O most sublime!

The world is wrapped
in yellow ribbons
of fear, knocked to its knees by the ox
of brutality.

The dead do not smell
in a camera's eye.
In a burned-out river bed
nobody cries.

The Temple of Baal
went down long ago.
The whores, the orchids, the eunuchs, the halls
    of elegance

    and the central way
    to the city of flowers
lie under four thousand years of sand.
    Now the barbarian

    calls on his god
to bomb the Tower of Babel again
    from the tall blue sky
while a million extras cry "Rhubarb!" to cover
    the sound of the fall.

Donald Revel

In the Alliance

Christmas lights too late in January
are bad jewels. They spoil the money.
The coming war comes too late to prevent
the dictatorship of the innocent.

Instructed by the highest school of aversion
in the deep nonsense of discipline,
the passionate lector
stays unarrested, untried here

mourning the death-cells as do I.
Their caucasian intimacies
and dreams the mortar-color of January
guarded the sun as lesser lights

who guarded the fine distinctions. In new war, none
accesses the wire and justice of what is gone.

William Stafford

Old Glory

No flag touched ours this year.
Our flag ate theirs. Ours cried,
"Banner, banner," all over the sky—
the sky now ours, the sea this year
our pond. "Thus far," we said,
"no farther," and the storm advanced,
or stopped, or hovered, depending.

We won, they say. They say good came:
we live in the shadow of our flag.
We fear no evil. Salute, ye people.
That feeling you have, they call it glory.
We own it now, they say, under God,
in the sky, on earth, as it is in heaven.

Maura Stanton

Sicence and Religion

January 1991

In grade school all knowledge fit together
Smoothly as the continents on the globe
When I spun the ball to watch the colors run.
I slid my Catechism inside my desk,
Between my fat, green History, and my thin
Geography with its slick maps and charts,
Then pulled my English book from underneath
To study grammar, or memorize poems
About Nature—skylarks and waterfowls—
Whose lines come back to me in snatches,
Like ironic subtitles, as the news flashes
Pictures of these dying cormorants
Trying to shake oil off their feathers,
And dolphins swimming away for their lives
While bombs light up the skies of Paradise,
That valley of the Tigris and Euphrates
Where Adam and Eve slept beside lions—
For even Paradise had boundaries
On the roll down Bible map that hung above
The blackboard, covering up other maps
Beneath it, the United States and Europe.
It seemed as much a place as any state,
No further from Peoria than Florida.

The maps rolled up, the blackboard clear again,
We'd turn to Math and Science after lunch.
Poor Adam's and Eve's many foolish children
Evolved into brutish stone age cavemen
Who had to rediscover Nature's laws.
I loved my illustrated Science book
And used to do experiments at home.
One spring I sieved up tadpoles from the pond,
Just as my book directed. I brought them home.
I smiled to watch the sleek little swimmers
Jet across my washtub and back again.
I'd created my own little world for them,
With maple leaves for islands, ferns for shade,
And one tall, fuzzy cattail for a flag.
I'd run home after school, forgetting homework
Sometimes stirring the water with my finger
To make them scoot faster like bobby pins.
But when the tadpoles hatched at last to frogs
And jumped over the side into the grass,
My triumph turned to horror. They all hopped
Underneath the porch. I couldn't reach them.
Their fresh skin withered, their small legs
Twitched helplessly, far from any water.
The book did not explain what new frogs ate.
I couldn't tempt them out with scraps of tuna
And when I sprayed them with the garden hose,
I drowned the ones who hadn't died of thirst.

Hunkering in the mud as buzzing flies
Began to flit over the collapsed bodies
Hardly distinguishable from clods or stones,

I felt confused and guilty. Above me
Indifferent clouds drifted through the sky
And I seemed alone for the first time,
Without a key to unlock the mystery
Of this disaster. No groveling prayer
could turn my mess into a miracle,
No bubbling beaker of chemicals, mixed
By the hand of the cleverest doctor,
Could make these frogs spring from the dead.
I'd like to say that's when I turned my back
On Science and Religion, but of course
I was afraid to think so boldly. Instead
My mother called me in for lunch; I ran
Away from what I'd done, forgot it,
Or almost forgot it, for the memory
Rises to the surface of my mind
As bombers strafe refineries in the desert
And blow up arsenals. The bat-like planes
Cast shadows across the sand where a snake
Still waits, coiled inside the Tree of Knowledge.

Terese Svoboda

Ajax's Mother

> *What is honor?*
> *A word.*
> —Falstaff

Two rivals, Homer tells me,
and dishonor. Honor

is a front for guilt,
therefore dishonor . . .

Something twists here,
a typical Greek lesson,

the writhing of a woman,
ten dead sheep. Enraged,

my son, without desiring it,
lays upon his sword, his name

spittle between consonants,
the luckless resonance

of blood. He wept, Homer says,
on a beach with gold drainage

for what the heart
gives out, which is not

honor. I say I gave him
life, Homer, you give his death

a name. He produces his lyre,
as usual. I consider the beach,

the rocks that cut my feet,
the smoking ash, the teeth

and fillings that make
enormous clatter after

and I ask: Homer, where
is honor? He pauses, pinches up

soot. Ajax, he says,
take off your helmet,

then he lets the specks
muddy the water,

the current swirling,
dropping, picking up.

Thom Tammaro

Thinking of the Tao Te Ching After the Persian Gulf War

Lao Tzu, I think of you at the gates of Chou near Han Ku Pass, twenty-five hundred years ago, saddened by the citizens of your country, weary of heart and without hope, writing down these words for the hopeful gatekeeper:

> *If you rejoice in victory, then you delight in killing:*
> *If you delight in killing, you cannot fulfill yourself.*
>
> ....
>
> *When many people are being killed,*
> *They should be mourned in heartfelt sorrow.*
> *That is why a victory must be observed like a funeral.*

Lao Tzu, I am sorry to report that we are still waiting for the generals to light the candles. We are still waiting for the victorious soldiers to carry the coffins of the enemy through the city gates. We have been praying for the dead when we should have been saving our prayers for the living. We have yet to learn how to celebrate victory. Coffin handles are still being carved from the hand bones of the dead.

Henry Taylor

Speech

1

I crouch over my radio
to tune in the President,
thinking how lucky I am
not to own a television.

2

Now the rich, cultivated voice
with its cautious, measured pauses
fills my living room, fills
the wastebasket, the vase
on the mantel, the hurricane
lamps, and even fills
the antique pottery whiskey jug
beside the fireplace, nourishing
the dried flowers I have put in it.

3

"I had a responsibility,"
he says; the phrase pours
from the speaker like molasses,
flows to the rug, spreads
into a black, shining puddle,
slowly expands, covers
the rug with dark sweetness.
It begins to draw flies;
they eat all the syrup
and clamor for more.

4

I can barely hear the speech
above the buzzing of their wings.
But the Commander in Chief
has the solution: another
phrase, sweeter, thicker,
blacker, oozes out
over my living room floor:
"I have personal reasons
for wanting peace." This is more
than the flies will be able to eat;
they will stay quiet
for the rest of the speech.

5

Now, you are thinking, comes
the Good Part, the part
where the syrup proves poisonous
and kills all the flies.
My fellow Americans, that
is not at all what happened.
The flies grew fat on the phrases,
grew as large as bullfrogs.

6

They are everywhere in the house,
and the syrup continues
to feed and fatten them:
in the pottery whiskey jug,
sprouting new leaves and buds,
even the dried flowers thrive.

7

The speech
has been over for weeks now;

they go on eating,
but they stay quiet
and seem peaceful enough.
At night, sometimes,
I can hear them
making soft liquid sounds
of contentment.

Jean Valentine

Butane

The huge aluminum airship
is gliding over us,
you and I with our children walking by Westport's
trees, seashore, gold trees, gold seashore.
I say, *what's that?* But no one sees it.
Then the second ship crashes just behind us,
spills butane lighter fluid over the field,
thinly spreading, fast, out over the next field;
we don't know, should we throw water over it
or not—which will be worse for the earth
(the earth itself isn't on fire yet,
only the corn in the field, and the next field).
The dwarf says, *Hold it!* walking up between my legs
into my body: *I'd better see the fire skin.*

Mark Vinz

Prairie Storm

Driving south from Winnipeg at night
we watch the border sky turn nightmare red.
All around us patches of fire and smoke
with scattered figures moving on the prairie.
A simple explanation, the customs agent says:
when the crops are in, the fields are burned.

To keep awake we listen to songs on the radio—
lost love and heartache, with bulletins of
world-wide storms, a threat of war continuing.
Easy enough to understand, isn't it?
After a harvest, what's left must burn.
All the long drive home we watch the sky for fire.

Ellen Bryant Voigt

The Innocents

Not as one might slip into a stream,
though it is a stream,
nor as we slide from sleep or into sleep,
but as the breath of a passing animal
unmoors a spore from the lacy frond
is the soul brought out of heaven.

It is another buoyancy.
With only the briefest fitfulness
the mote hangs in the vapor above the pond,
the crumb rides at the end of the supple line
on the skin of the river
until the slick fish swallows.

  One fish, two fish, how many of God's fish
  swam out to sea?

  Muskrat, mud rat, does the toothed water rat
  still hunt in the sea?

  Night bird, nested bird, who drew the whistling bird
  so far from the sea?

  Red fox, brown fox, can any hungry silver fox
  remember the sea?

Robert Wallace

The Stone

What must it do
as morning drains
away; then noon,
and afternoon?

Leaves flutter, dusk
draws out the shadows.

O busy stone!
It holds its place.

Marilyn Nelson Waniek

Matins (2:30 A.M.)

One-third of the world
is dreaming right now of food.
Another third stares
into empty handmade bowls,
and I can't sleep
for indigestion.

Is this pain heartburn,
or the posthumous reason
for my incomprehensible death?
They die
anonymous:
Sudanese children.
Lebanese mother
holding her limp, long baby.
Decimated villagers.

They cry,
What can I have done
to deserve this pain?
This soul-killing fear?

And my meshuggenah fear.
That so many should hunger while I promise

never again to Really Eat The Whole Thing;
that they should sleep in the open wind
while I hope for posthumous anthology fame;
that they should need
while I lie wondering
how long it will take my husband
to drive me to the emergency room,
and how to spell relief.
Jesus. I must be the smallest grain
of salt of the earth.

Michael Waters

The Torches

Nicaragua

Limbs lopped off, the fathers
thrashed through the orchard
till a torch was touched to their hair
and they were consumed by the unearthly
love that lifted their souls toward heaven.
How impossible to mute the body with belief.
Women closed their shutters and crossed themselves.
Soldiers jeered. But the burning were beyond
the grievous clamor of the New World.

Clear sky that night, the thousand stars
assuming tentative shapes
like children assembling in the schoolyard.
The ashes smoldered on the hillside.
Then rain. By morning, only chipped dice and the
        scorched soil remained.

What's irrefutable is that sweeping odor,
not the fume of charred tongues and gasoline,
but the first profuse blossoming of orchids,
a fragrant exhalation from the earth's core,
and those sudden shafts of light
crisscrossing in the late afternoon
as the missing bear through the marketplace
their flaming tapers of spine, their wicks of hair.

C. D. Wright

Song Of The Gourd

In gardening I continued to sit on my side of the car to drive
whenever possible at the usual level of distraction in
gardening I shat nails glass contaminated dirt and threw up
on the new shoots in gardening I learned to praise things I
had dreaded I pushed the hair out of my face I felt less
responsible for one man's death one woman's longterm
isolation my bones softened in gardening I lost nickels and
ring setting I uncovered buttons and marbles I lay half the
worm aside and sought the rest I sought myself in the bucket
and wondered why I came into being in the first place in
gardening I turned away from the television and went around
smelling of offal the inedible parts of the chicken in
gardening I said excelsior in gardening I required no
company I had to forgive my own failure to perceive how
things were between them since I was not privileged I went
out barelegged at dusk and dug and dug and dug for a better
understanding I hit rock my ovaries softened in gardening I
was protean as in no other realm before or since I longed to
torch my old belongings to belch a little flame of satisfaction
in gardening I longed to stroll farther into soundlessness I
could almost forget what happened many swift years ago in
arkansas I felt like a god from down under chthonian in
gardening I thought this is it body and soul I am home at

last excelsior praise the grass in gardening I fled the fold
that supported the war only in gardening could I stop
shrieking stop stop the slaughter only in gardening could I
press my ear to the ground to hear my soul let out an
unyielding noise my lines softened I turned the water onto
the joyfilled boy child only in gardening did I feel fit to
partake to go on trembling in the last light I confess the
abject urge to weed your beds while the bittersweet
overwhelmed my day lilies I summoned the courage to grin I
climbed the hill with my bucket and slept like a dipper in
the cool of your body besotted with growth infected by green

Jean Zaleski

"The Vise"

Notes on Contributors

Joan Aleshire has published two books of poems, *Cloud Train* (Texas Tech, 1982) and *This Far* (Quarterly Review Poetry Series, 1987). She teaches in the MFA program at Warren Wilson College in Vermont.

Dick Allen's books of poetry include *Flight and Pursuit* and *Overnight in the Guest House of the Mystic*, both published by LSU Press. Among his honors is an NEA grant. His work has appeared in *The Best American Poetry 1991*, *The New Yorker*, and *Poetry*.

John Allman has published four books of poems, the latest being *Curve Away from Stillness* (New Directions, 1989). His poem presented here will be in his fifth book, *The Expulsions*.

Jim Barnes edits *The Chariton Review* at Northeast Missouri State University. His seventh book of poems, *The Sawdust War*, will come out this spring from the University of Illinois Press. He is the translator of Dagmar Nick, a contemporary German poet.

Marvin Bell did a tour in the U.S. Army in the mid-Sixties. He has published many books of poetry, the latest being *Iris of Creation* (Cooper Canyon, 1990) and *New and Selected Poems* (Atheneum, 1987). He lives in Iowa City, Iowa, and Port Townsend, Washington.

Michael Benedikt's fifth collection of poetry is the *Badminton at Great Barrington* (Univ. of Pittsburgh Press, 1980). *Night Cries, Mole Notes, Sky*, and *The Body* were published by Wesleyan. He recently videotaped a reading of his verse and prose for the Library of Congress.

Robert Bly saw the publication of his *Selected Poems* (Harper and Row) in 1986 and of *A Little Book on the Human Shadow* in 1988. He is recently represented by his book, *Iron John*.

Philip Booth, who lives in Maine, taught for many years at Syracuse University. His recent books of poetry are *Relations* (Viking, 1986) and *Selves* (Viking, 1990).

Michael Dennis Browne's fourth collection of poems, *You Won't Remember This*, is being published this winter by Carnegie-Mellon University Press. He teaches at the University of Minnesota.

Amy Clampitt was born and brought up in rural Iowa. Her books of poetry include, most recently, *Westward*, published by Knopf.

Richard A. Clark, painter and lithographer, holds an MFA from Syracuse and taught at Miami in Ohio. His work is in many private and public collections, including the Boston Public Library. A Vermont resident, he was among the founders of the radical Liberty Union Party.

Jane Cooper has published three books of poems, including *Scaffolding: New and Selected Poems* (Anvil Press Poetry, London) which contains the complete text of "Threads: Rosa Luxemburg from Prison." Her recent work is in *APR, The New Yorker,* and *Kenyon Review.*

Jayne Cortez, born in Arizona, now lives in New York City. Her eight books and five recordings include, most recently, *Poetic Magnetic* and *Everywhere Drums.* Recipient of an American Book Award, she has presented her poetry throughout Africa, Europe, and the Americas.

Philip Dacey has published *How I Escaped from the Labyrinth, The Boy Under the Bed,* and *The Man with Red Suspenders* (Milkweed Editions, 1986). He teaches at Southwest State University in Marshall, Minnesota.

Diana Der-Hovanessian is the author of twelve books of poetry, including *About Time* and *Songs of Bread, Songs of Salt* (Ashod Press, 1987, 1990), and of translations, including the award-winning *Anthology of Armenian Poetry* (Columbia University Press, 1978) and *Land of Fire* (Ardis).

Stephen Dunn has recently published Landscape at the End of the Century, *Between Angels,* and *Local Time.* He is widely anthologized in collections that include *New American Poets of the '90s.*

Clayton Eshleman published three books in 1989: *Cro-Magnon* (Black Sparrow), *Antiphonal Swing: Selected prose 1962-1987* (McPherson & Co.), and *Novices: a Study of Poetic Apprenticeship* (Mercer & Aitchison). He teaches at Eastern Michigan University where he edits *Sulfur.*

David Ferry, who teaches at Wellesley College, most recently published *Strangers: a Book of Poems* (University of Chicago Press, 1983). This spring Farrar, Straus and Giroux will bring out *Gilgamesh: a New Rendering in English Verse.*

Roland Flint's books of poems include *Resuming Green: Selected Poems 1965-1982* (Dial Press, 1983). He teaches at Georgetown University.

Reginald Gibbons, the editor of *TriQuarterly* magazine, has recently published his poems, *Maybe It Was So* (Univ. of Chicago Press) and a book of very short stories, *Five Pears or Peaches* (Broken Moon Press).

Allen Ginsberg, who has had poems recently in *Esquire, Vanity Fair* and the *Nation,* is author of many books, including *White Shroud Poems 1980-1986* and *Howl, Annotated,* both from Harper and Row.

Diane Glancy teaches Native American literature and creative writing at Macalester College. Her poetry collections include *Lone Dog's Winter Count* (West End Press, 1991), *Offering* (Holy Cow! Press, 1988), and *One Age in a Dream* (Milkweed Editions, 1986).

Patricia Goedicke, who teaches in the University of Montana writing program, is the author of *Listen, Love* (Barnwood) and *The Tongues We*

Speak: New and Selected Poems (Milkweed Editions, 1989).

Albert Goldbarth's most recent collection of poems is *Heaven and Earth* (University of Georgia Press, 1991). He lives in Wichita, Kansas, where he is Distinguished Professor of Humanities at Wichita State University.

Donald Hall's *The One Day* won the National Book Critics Circle Award and *The Los Angeles Times* Book Prize. His books of poetry and commentary include *Kicking the Leaves* and *Poetry and Ambition.*

Sam Hamill, editor at Copper Canyon Press, spent the weeks of Desert Storm translating Matsuo Bosho's *Narrow Road to the Interior.* New Directions published his translations from ancient Greek, *The Infinite Moment,* and Milkweed Editions, his book of poems, *Mandala.*

Linda M. Hasselstrom writes from Hermosa, South Dakota. Her works include *Roadkill* (Spoon River) and *Going Over East: Reflections of a Woman Rancher* (Fulcrum).

William Heyen, professor SUNY – Brockport, has received Guggenheim, NEA and American Academy-National Institute awards. He is the author of *Erika: Poems of the Holocaust, Pterodactyl Rose: Poems of Ecology, Ribbons: the Gulf War,* and *The Host: Selected Poems 1965-1990.*

Jonathan Holden's books of poetry and criticism include the *Names of the Rapids* and *Against Paradise. The Fate of Latin American Poetry, American Gothic,* and a novel, *Brilliant Kinds* are due this year. He teaches at Kansas State University.

Bill Holm lives in Minneota, Minnesota, and has taught in schools in the U.S., Iceland, and China. He has four books, two of poems—*Boxelder Bug Variations* and *The Dead Get by with Everything*—and two of prose— *The Music of Failure* and *Coming Home Crazy* (Milkweed Editions).

Edwin Honig has translated classical Spanish and Portuguese literature, anthologized American poets, and published a dozen books of his own poetry from *The Moral Circus* and the *Gazebos* (1955, 1961) to *Interrupted Praise: New/Selected Poems* (1983).

Colette Inez is the author of *Eight Minutes From the Sun* (Saturday Press, 1983) and *Family Life* (Story Line Press, 1988). She lives in New York City and is working on a one-act opera on the life of Mary Shelley.

Dale Jacobson from Minnesota is the author of *Poems for Goya's Disparates* (Jazz Press, 1980) and *Shouting at Midnight* (Spirit Horse Press, 1986), a long poem in part about the war against Vietnam.

J. Kates is a poet, translator and writer who lives in Fitzwilliam, New Hampshire. His work has appeared in *Hawaii Review, Cypher, Oxford Magazine, Z Miscellaneous, New York Quarterly,* and other journals.

Edward Kleinschmidt, assistant professor at Santa Clara, has had poems in *APR, The Gettysburg Review, The New Yorker,* and *Best American*

Poetry 1990. His poetry books are *Magnetism* (Heyeck Press, 1988) and *First Language* (University of Massachusetts Press, Juniper Prize, 1989).

Wendy Wilder Larsen's book of narrative verse *Shallow Graves: Two Women and Vietnam* was published by Random House. She has had poems in such magazines as *The Paris Review*, *Seattle* and *Nimrod* and is on the Board of Poets House.

Denise Levertov lives in Seattle and teaches each winter at Stanford University. The poem presented here will be in her next book, coming out later this year from New Directions, publisher also of her *New and Selected Essays*.

Philip Levine, a native of Detroit living in California and presently teaching in New York City, is the author of *Selected Poems* and *Sweet Will* (Atheneum 1984, 1985) and recently of *New and Selected Poems* and *What Work Is* (Knopf, 1991), winner of the National Book Award.

Thomas Lux, who teaches at Sarah Lawrence College, is the author of *Sunday* (1979) and *Half Promised Land* (1986) as well as the recent *The Drowned River*, all from Houghton Mifflin.

Dan Masterson's third volume of poetry, *World Without End*, was recently published by the University of Arkansas Press. He has received two Pushcart prizes, a Borestone Award, the *Poetry Northwest* Bullis prize, and a CCLM Fels Award.

Cleopatra Mathis is the author of *Aerial View of Louisiana* and *The Bottom Land* (Sheep Meadow Press, 1980, 1983). She lives in New Hampshire and teaches at Dartmouth.

Mekeel McBride has four cats, one dog, two aquariums and poems recently in *North American Review*, *Seneca*, *Grand Street*, and *California Quarterly*. Carnegie-Mellon University Press publishes her work, including her next, fourth book, *The Mole of Life*.

Jay Meek is publishing *Windows*, his fifth book of poems with Carnegie-Mellon University Press, this year. He teaches at the University of North Dakota where he is editor for *North Dakota Quarterly*.

Nelson Moe, translator and specialist in Italian literature, has written about Scotellaro and Gramsci and recently, on the war poetry of Amelia Roselli (Italica). He also translated *The Myth of the Other: Lacan, Deleuze, Foucault, Bataille* (Maisonneuve Press).

James Moore, whose most recent book is *The Freedom of History* (Milkweed Editions, 1988), offers three selections from a book-length poem. The Rilke quote is from *Letters to a Young Poet*. The other is from section 5 of Miguel Hernandez's *The Unending Lightning*.

Lisel Mueller has published *The Need to Hold Still* and *Second Language* with Louisiana State University Press and, most recently, also with

LSU Press, *Waving from the Shore*. She lives in Lake Forest, Illinois.

Carol Muske teaches in the English Department of the University of Southern California. Her new book is *Red Trousseau* (Viking), and follows her *Dear Digby* (Viking, 1981), *Applause and Wyndmere* (University of Pittsburgh Press 1989, 1985).

Kathleen Norris, author of *Middle of the World* (University of Pittsburgh Press, 1981) and a South Dakota resident, is spending this year at the Ecumenical Research Institute of St. John's University of Minnesota.

Sharon Olds teaches at New York University and Goldwater Hospital. Her books of poetry include *The Dead & the Living* (1984), *The Gold Cell* (1987), and *The Father* (Spring, 1992), all from Alfred A. Knopf.

Walter Pavlich's collections include *Ongoing Portraits*, a Pushcart Writers' Choice selection, and forthcoming from the University of Iowa Press, *Running Near the End of the World*, winner of the San Francisco Foundation Jackson Award and the Edwin Ford Piper Poetry Award.

Molly Peacock lives in New York City and is president of the Poetry Society of America. Her books include *Raw Heaven* and *Take Heart* (Random House, 1984, 1989).

E. S. Reeve, painter, has shown in Boston, New Hope, and New England galleries. Her work is in private collections in the U.S. and Europe.

F. D. Reeve's recent work includes *The White Monk: an Essay on Dostoyevsky and Melville*, *The Garden: New and Selected Poetry and the Prose by Bella Akhmadulina*, and *Concrete Music*.

Donald Revell is author of four volumes of poetry, including *From the Abandoned Cities* (Harper & Row) and the *Gaze of Winter* (University of Georgia Press). He is the editor of *Denver Quarterly*.

David Shapiro is an artist and art historian, author of *Social Realism: Art as a Weapon* and *American Images in Twentieth-Century Art*. His work is in the permanent collections of the Metropolitan, the Smithsonian, and other national museums.

William Stafford, a Kansan now living in Oregon, has taught in colleges throughout the West and served as Poetry Consultant for the Library of Congress. A conscientious objector in World War II, he is the author most recently of *An Oregon Message* and *Passwords* (Harper Collins.

Maura Stanton teaches at Indiana University. Her third book of poetry, *Tales of the Supernatural*, was published by David R. Godine in 1988. Her second book, *Cries of Swimmers*, was recently reprinted in Carnegie-Mellon's Classic Contemporary Series.

Terese Svoboda has recently brought out *Cleaned the Crocodile's Teeth* (Greenfield Review Press) and *All Aberration* (University of Georgia Press). Her *Laughing Africa* won the 1989 Iowa Poetry Prize. She specializes in designing and directing video presentations of poetry.

Thom Tammaro teaches writing and humanities at Moorhead State University. He has edited *Rowing Across Fields: a Conversation with William Stafford* and *Uncollected Poems 1942-1982* and *Common Ground: Poems on Rural Life.*

Henry Taylor, awarded a Pulitzer prize for his book *The Flying Change* (Louisiana University Press, 1985), wrote *An Afternoon of Pocket Billiards* (University of Utah Press, 1975) to be reprinted by LSU this spring along with *The Horse Show at Midnight.*

Jean Valentine, born in Chicago, has published five collections of poetry, most recently *Home, Deep, Blue, New & Selected Poems* (Alice James Books, 1989), which won the Maurice English Poetry Prize. She teaches at Sarah Lawrence College and the West Side Y.

Mark Vinz will have two collections of poems published in 1992: *Minnesota Gothic* (Milkweed Editions) and *Late Night Calls* (New Rivers Press). He edits Dakota Territory Press.

Ellen Bryant Voigt has published three volumes of poetry—*Claiming Kin* (1976), *The Forces of Plenty* (1983), and *The Lotus Flowers* (1987). *Two Trees*, her fourth volume, is due from W. W. Norton this fall. An NEA and Guggenheim grantee, she teaches at Warren Wilson College.

Robert Wallace's most recent book is *The Common Summer: New And Selected Poems* (Carnegie-Mellon University Press). He is the author also of *Writing Poems* (Little, Brown). He teaches in Cleveland.

Marilyn Nelson Waniek's books are *For the Body* (1978), *Mama's Promises* (1985), and *The Homeplace* (1990), all published by Louisiana State University Press. Married and the mother of two, she is a professor of English at the University of Connecticut.

Michael Waters teaches at Salisbury State University. His books—all from Carnegie-Mellon University Press—are *Anniversary of the Air* (1985), *The Burden Lifters* (1989), and *Bountiful* (due this year). In 1986 he participated in the Al-Merbid Poetry Festival in Baghdad.

C. D. Wright is the author of *Further Adventures with You* (Carnegie-Mellon University Press, 1985). Her poem presented here is from a MS in progress titled "Tremble." She teaches at Brown University.

Jean Zaleski, painter, a native of Malta, long resident in New York City, whose work hangs in many private and public collections, has presented "Treespaces," "Magic Mountains," and, last fall, "Megaliths and Malta." Reproduced here is a work from her "Man sEries."

Acknowledgments

"The Peaceable Sleepers; or, Poem to be Read Before, During, and After any of These 'Truly Nauseating Wars,' That, Truly, 'Make Everybody Sick'" appeared in an earlier version in *Field* and in *Am Here Forum*, © Michael Benedikt. By permission of the author.

"Fragments" is reprinted from "Threads: Rosa Luxemburg from Prison" © 1979 by Jane Cooper.

"The Coalition" first appeared in *The Nation*, © by Donald Hall.

"The Truth," section 38 from *Ribbons: the Gulf War*, © 1991 by Timeless Press. By permission of Time Being Books.

"A Rabbit Snared in a Fence of Pain," section 2 from "To My God in His Sickness," from *The Names of the Lost*, © 1976 by Philip Levine.

"The Protestor" appeared first in *The Paris Review*, © by Sharon Olds.

"Speech" © 1975 by Henry Taylor, Reprinted by permission of the author from *An Afternoon of Pocket Billiards* (University of Utah Press, 1975).

"The Innocents" appeared first in *Erato: Harvard Book Review*, 19-20 (1991), © by Ellen Bryant Voigt.

"The Stone" reprinted from *The Formalist*, © by Robert Wallace.

"Matins" first appeared in *The Kenyon Review*, 13.3 (Summer 1991), © by Marilyn Nelson Waniek.